PRAYERS

AND

OTHER DEVOTIONS

FOR THE

USE OF THE SOLDIERS

OF THE

ARMY OF THE CONFEDERATE STATES

CHARLESTON, S. C.

PUBLISHED FOR

FEMALE BIBLE, PRAYER-BOOK AND TRACT SOCIETY

Evans & Cogswell, Printers, No. 3 Broad Street

REPRINTED BY

Wake Forest, NC
www.scuppernongpress.com

Prayers And Other Devotions For The Use Of The Soldiers Of The Army Of The Confederate States

By Female Bible, Prayer-Book and Tract Society
Foreword by Rev. Dr. Herman White

©2018 The Scuppernong Press

First Printing

The Scuppernong Press
PO Box 1724
Wake Forest, NC 27588
www.scuppernongpress.com

Cover and book design by Frank B. Powell, III

All rights reserved

Printed in the United States of America

No part of this book may be reproduced or transmitted in any form or by any means, electronic or mechanical, including photocopying, recording, or by any information and storage and retrieval system, without written permission from the editor and/or publisher.

International Standard Book Number
ISBN 978-1-942806-16-5

Library of Congress Control Number:
2018941304

Contents

Introduction i

Foreword iii

Selections From The Psalms 1

The Soldier's Prayer in Camp 7

Prayers to be Used Before Battle 11

A Thanksgiving after Victory 13

Prayer to be used by a Sick or Wounded
  Soldier 15

Just as I Am 18

Thy Will Be Done 19

Sun of My Soul! 21

Introduction

This small 12-page prayer book was originally published in Charleston, SC, early in the War to be distributed to Confederate soldiers marching off to war or already in the field.

As you will read on the next page, in the excellent foreword by Rev. Dr. Herman White, this was a common practice across the South throughout the conflict as soldiers were desperate to hear the word of God.

This yearning intensified later as great revivals swept the Southern armies during the winters of 1863 and 1864. Hopefully, this small prayer book played a part in bringing comfort to the men in the field as they faced the horrors of war.

The original book was set in very small type and hard to read, so our reprint has been reset larger in a modern typeface with all the original language intact.

We hope you enjoy our efforts.

— *Frank B. Powell, III, Editor*

Foreword

As a college student in world history, I learned that cultures from antiquity have centered in the worship of a god. Although they might have a pantheon of false gods, there was always the primary deity which was the bedrock of their culture.

The bedrock of the Southern American culture was that the Bible was indeed the infallible word of the God who created the heavens, the earth, and all that is therein; and that Jesus Christ is the only means of redemption. Therefore, it should not be surprising to anyone, that at the beginning of the War of Northern Aggression many of the political, military officers, and soldiers were Christians. As a result they knew the great need for those going into battle to possess the Bible, New Testaments, tracts, and hymn books, especially for those who were unsaved.

Nearly all of the publishers of Bibles, New Testaments, and tracts were located in the north when the war broke out. And the northern societies "generally declared Bibles and Testaments "contraband of war," and we had at once to face the problem of securing (them) through the blockade, or manufacturing them with our poor facilities." (1)

It was simply amazing how politicians, army commanders, preachers, churches, chaplains, and the people of the Confederacy immediately set into motion whatever was necessary to supply the troops with God's word. Many risked their lives running the blockade, others even borrowed money to pay publishers in England for Bibles. Some in the South actually took the wallpaper down for printers to use. It would require many pages to give the testimonies to the success of their effort. But even during that awful war as the Confederates fought for their sovereign States against the northern invaders it is not surprising that great revivals broke out in their armies. From October 4, 1862, when it began, until the end of the war the revival fires continued to burn, and more than

150,000 were documented as being saved. To God be the glory!

In closing I have in my possession a pocket hymn book that my grandfather, Pvt. David Edward White, Co. G, 21st Regiment, N. C. Troops carried. It is missing the first few pages, but starts with hymn 13 through hymn 264. The title at the top of each page is "Prayer Meeting Hymns" and my father said that his father told him it was a Methodist Book of Songs. Suffice it to say that these Bibles, tracts and song books were greatly treasured by the troops in the greatest army which ever marched against invading heathen. Thank God for a heritage passed to us from people who were God fearing, and God loving!

Rev. Dr. W. Herman White, Chaplain

North Carolina Division
Sons of Confederate Veterans and the

Army of Northern Virginia Department,
Sons of Confederate Veterans

PRAYERS

AND

OTHER DEVOTIONS

FOR THE

USE OF THE SOLDIERS

OF THE

ARMY OF THE CONFEDERATE STATES

PRAYERS, AND OTHER DEVOTIONS

SELECTIONS FROM THE PSALMS

The Lord is my light and my salvation, whom, then, shall I fear?

The Lord is the strength of my life, of whom, then, shall I be afraid?

When the wicked, even mine enemies and my foes, came upon me to eat up my flesh, they stumbled and fell.

Though an host of men were laid against me, yet shall not my heart be afraid; and though there rose up war against me, yet will I put my trust in Thee.

One thing have I desired of the Lord, which I will require, even that I may dwell in the house of the Lord all the days of my life, to behold the fair beauty of the Lord, and to visit His temple.

For in the time of trouble He shall hide me in His tabernacle; yea, in the secret place of His dwelling shall He hide me, and set me up upon a rock of stone.

And now shall He lift up mine head above mine enemies round about me. Therefore will I offer in His dwelling an oblation, with great gladness; I will sing and speak praises unto the Lord.

Hearken unto my voice, O Lord, when I cry unto Thee; have mercy upon me and hear me.

My heart hath talked of Thee. Seek ye my face: Thy face, Lord, will I seek.

O hide not Thou thy face from me, nor cast Thy servant away in displeasure.

Thou hast been my succor; leave me not, neither forsake me, O God of my salvation.

When my father and my mother forsake me, the Lord taketh me up.

Teach me Thy way, O Lord, and lead me in the right way because of mine enemies.

Deliver me not over into the will of mine adversaries: for there are false witnesses risen up against me, and such as speak wrong.

I should utterly have fainted, but that I believe verily to see the goodness of the Lord in the land of the living.

O tarry thou the Lord's leisure; be strong and He shall comfort thine heart; and put thou thy trust in the, Lord.

The angel of the Lord tarrieth round about them that fear Him, and delivereth them.

The eyes of the Lord are over the righteous, and His ears are open unto their prayers.

The countenance of the Lord is against them that do evil, to root out the remembrance of them from the earth.

The righteous cry, and the Lord heareth them and delivereth them out of all their troubles.

The Lord is nigh unto them that are of a contrite heart, and will save such as be of an humble spirit.

Plead Thou my cause, O Lord, with them that strive with me, and fight Thou against them that fight against me.

Lay hand upon the shield and buckler, and stand up to help me.

Bring forth the spear, and stop the way against them that persecute me; say unto my soul, I am thy salvation.

Whoso dwelleth under the defence of the Most High, shall abide under the shadow of the Almighty.

I will say unto the Lord, Thou art my hope and my stronghold; my God, in Him will I trust.

For He shall deliver thee from the snare of the hunter, and from the noisome pestilence.

He shall defend thee under His wings, and thou shalt be safe under His feathers; His faithfulness and truth shall be thy shield and buckler.

Thou shalt not be afraid for any terror by night, nor for the arrow that flieth by day; for the pestilence that walketh in darkness, nor for the sickness that destroyeth in the noon-day.

A thousand shall fall beside thee, and ten thousand at thy right hand, but it shall not come nigh thee.

Yea, with thine eyes shalt thou behold, and see the reward of the ungodly.

For Thou, Lord, art my hope; Thou hast set thine house of defence very high.

The Lord sitteth above the water flood, and the Lord remaineth a king for ever.

The Lord shall give strength unto His people; the Lord shall give His people the blessing of peace.

———————

The Soldier's Prayer in Camp.

O Eternal God, who by Thy unsearchable wisdom, by Thy Almighty power and secret providence, dost determine the issues of human counsels, the events of war and the return of victory and peace, let the light of Thy countenance, and the blessed influences of Thy mercy, be once more shed upon this afflicted land. Pity the evils which we suffer under the power and tyranny of war, and although we acknowledge Thy justice in our sufferings and adore Thee in thy judgments, yet we beseech Thee to hearken to our prayers and provide a remedy for our calamities. Let not the defenders of a righteous cause go away ashamed, nor their counsels be brought to nought. Look with compassion upon our infirmities and remember not our sins, but support us with Thy staff, lift us up with Thy hand, and refresh us with Thy presence. And if a threatening cloud should still overshadow us, illuminate our minds with divine truth, that with tho eye of faith and hope we may see beyond it; catching a glimpse of those mercies which in Thy secret providence and adorable wisdom Thou mayest still vouchsafe to Thy unworthy servants amidst the saddening scenes and hardships of war.

Give us grace and strength diligently to do our duty and cheerfully to submit to Thy will; and as we do put our whole trust and confidence in Thy mercy, and have laid up all our hopes in Thy bosom, let us never be put to shame or confusion before our enemies: but as Thine are the strength and the power, Lord of Hosts, do

Thou make bare Thy mighty arm and give us the victory. Place a guard of angels, O Lord, about the Commander-in-chief, and uphold him with the defence of Thy right hand, that no unhallowed arm may do him violence; support him in all his dangers and trials, and give to all under his orders the spirit of confidence and obedience. Bless all the subordinate officers and confederates under his command. Direct their counsels, govern their actions, unite their hearts and strengthen their bands. Inspire all in the army with ready submission to lawful authority, with a sense of justice and integrity in all their dealings; with courage to resist and overcome the furiousness of our enemies; with compassion to spare the vanquished, and with a ready will to protect the oppressed; that approving themselves to Thee, the Almighty Ruler and Sovereign Disposer of all things, they may receive a full reward for their fidelity and obedience, and, at last, the gift of eternal life, through Jesus Christ our Lord!

Amen.

Prayers to be used before Battle.

O Most Powerful and glorious Lord God, the Lord of hosts, that rulest and commandest all things; Thou sittest in the throne judging right: and, therefore, we make our address to thy Divine Majesty, in this our necessity, that Thou wouldst take the cause into thine own hand, and judge between us and our enemies. Stir up thy strength, O Lord, and come and help us; for Thou givest not always the battle to the strong, but canst save by many or by few. O let not our sins now cry against us for vengeance; but hear us, thy poor servants, begging mercy, and imploring thy help, and that Thou wouldst be a defence unto us against the face of the enemy; make it appear that Thou art our Saviour and mighty

Deliverer, through Jesus Christ our Lord.

Amen.

Lord be merciful to us sinners, and save us for thy mercy's sake.

Thou art the great God, who hast made and rulest all things: O, deliver us for thy name's sake.

Thou art the great God to be feared above all: O save us, that we may praise thee.

Thou, O Lord, art just and powerful: O defend our cause against the face of the enemy

O God, thou art a strong tower of defence to all who fly unto thee: O save us from the violence of the enemy.

O Lord of Hosts, fight for us ; that we may glorify thee.

O suffer us not to sink under the weight of our sins, or the violence of the enemy.

O Lord, arise, help us, and deliver us, for thy name's sake.

Amen.

A Thanksgiving after Victory.

O Almighty God, the Sovereign Commander of all the world, in whose hand is power and might, which none is able to withstand ; we bless and magnify thy great and glorious name for this happy victory, the whole glory whereof we do ascribe to thee, who art the only giver of victory. And, we beseech thee, give us grace to improve this great mercy to thy glory, the advancement of thy Gospel, the honor of our country, and, as much as in us lieth, to the good of all mankind.

And, we beseech thee, give us such a sense of this great mercy, as may engage us to a true thankfulness, such as may appear in our lives, by an humble, holy, and obedient walking before thee all our days, through Jesus Christ our Lord: to whom, with thee, and the Holy Spirit, as for all thy mercies, so in particular for this victory and deliverance, be all glory and honor, world without end.

Amen.

Our Father, who art in Heaven, hallowed be Thy name; Thy kingdom come; Thy will be done on earth, as it is in Heaven; give us this day our daily bread; and forgive us our trespasses, as we forgive those who trespass against us; and lead us not into temptation, but deliver us from evil; for thine is the kingdom, the power and the glory, for ever and ever.
Amen.

2 Cor. xiii, 14.

The grace of our Lord Jesus Christ, and the love of God, and the fellowship of the Holy Ghost, be with us all evermore.
Amen.

———

Prayer to be used by a Sick or Wounded Soldier.

O, Almighty God, Father of men and angels, in whose hands are the keys of life and death, to whom it belongs justly to punish sinners, and to be merciful to those who truly repent, look down in great mercy on me, Thy unworthy servant, now suffering sickness and pain, which Thou in Thy wise providence has sent upon me.

Thou hast commanded us to call upon Thee in our trouble, and hast promised to deliver us. Give me grace to rely with unshaken confidence on Thy glorious promises. O, leave me not, nor forsake me, for there is none that can help or deliver, but only Thou, O God.

In Thee, Lord, do I put my trust, let me never be confounded. Give me patience and resignation, a perfect abandonment of my own will and a conformity to thine, that I may be prepared to endure evil at Thy hand with fortitude, or to receive good with thankfulness. But yet, O Lord my God, give Thy servant leave to pray unto Thee, that Thou wilt not cut me off in the midst of my days, nor forsake me when my strength faileth. Spare me, O God, that I may live to serve Thee, to redeem my time misspent in folly, to gain victory over my temptations, and perfect dominion over my passions. O spare me a little, that I may recover my strength before I go hence and be no more seen; so shall Thy servant rejoice in Thy mercies, and speak of Thy loving-kindness in the church of the redeemed.

Give me true repentance for all my sins. Enable me steadfastly to believe in Jesus Christ the Lamb of God, which taketh away the sins of the world. Let me be washed, let me be sanctified, let me be justified in the name of the Lord Jesus, and by Thy Spirit, O Lord God. Make me meet, by the renewing of the Holy Ghost, for the inheritance of Thy saints, that if it shall be Thy pleasure to take away my life by this visitation, I may rest in Jesus, or if Thou shalt be pleased in Thy mercy, to raise me up from this bed of languishing, I may always remember Thy goodness, and carry with me, through all my days, the impressions which Thy grace has now made upon me, and, by Thy help, joyfully serve Thee to thine honor and the salvation of my own soul, through Jesus Christ our Lord, in whose name alone I present my prayer to Thee.

Come unto me all ye that labor and are heavy laden, and I will give you rest. Take my yoke upon you and learn of me ; for I am meek and lowly in heart, and ye shall find rest for your souls, for my yoke is easy and my burden is light. — Matt, xi, 28, 29, 30.

For God so loved the world, that he gave his only begotten Son, that whosoever believeth in Him should not perish, but have everlasting life. — John, iii, 16.

This is a true saying, and worthy of all acceptation, that Christ Jesus came into the world to save sinners, of whom I am chief. — 1 Tim. i, 15.

If any man sin, we have an advocate with the Father, Jesus Christ, the righteous; and he is the propitiation for our sins. — 1 John, ii, 1, 2.

Just as I am, without one plea,
But that thy blood was shed for me,
And that thou bid'st me come to thee,
    O Lamb of God! I come.

Just as I am, and waiting not,
To rid my soul of one dark blot,
To thee whose blood can cleanse each spot,
    O Lamb of God! I come.

Just as I am, though tossed about,
With many a conflict, many a doubt,
"Fighting within and fears without,"
    O Lamb of God! I come.

Just as I am — poor, wretched, blind,
Sight, riches, healing of the mind —
Yea, all I want in thee to find:
    O Lamb of God! I come.

Just as I am, thou wilt receive,
Wilt welcome, pardon, cleanse, relieve;
Because thy promise I believe,
    O Lamb of God! I come.

Just as I am — thy love unknown,
Has broken every barrier down;
Now to be thine, yea thine alone,
    O Lamb of God! I come.

THY WILL BE DONE.

My God, my Father, while I stray
Far from my home on life's rough way,
Oh! teach me from my heart to say,
    "Thy will be done."

Though dark my path, and sad my lot,
May I be still, and murmur not,
But breathe the prayer divinely taught—
    "Thy will be done."

What though in lonely grief I sigh
For friends beloved, no longer nigh?
Submissive still I would reply,
    "Thy will be done."

If Thou should'st call me to resign
What most I prize — it ne'er was mine,
I only yield thee what is thine!
    "Thy will be done."

E'en if again I ne'er should see
The friend more dear than life to me,
Ere long we both shall be with thee —
    "Thy will be done."

Should pining sickness waste away
My life in premature decay,
My Father, still I strive to say,
    "Thy will be done."

If but my fainting heart be blest,
With thy sweet Spirit for its guest,
My God, to thee I leave the rest —
    "Thy will be done."

Renew my will from day to day,
Blend it with thine and take away
All that now makes it hard to say
    "Thy will be done."

And when on earth I breathe no more,
The prayer oft mixed with tears before,
I'll sing upon a happier shore,
    "Thy will be done;"

Sun of my soul! Thou Saviour dear,
It is not night if thou be near:
O may no earth-born cloud arise
To hide thee from thy servant's eyes.

When the soft dews of kindly sleep
My wearied eyelids gently steep,
Be my last thought, how sweet to rest
Forever on my Saviour's breast.

Abide with me from morn till eve,
For without thee I cannot live:
Abide with me when night is nigh,
For without thee I dare not die.

Watch by the sick; enrich the poor
With blessings from thy boundless store;
Be every mourner's sleep to-night
Like infants' slumbers, pure and light.

Come near and bless us when we wake,
Ere through the world our way we take:
Till in the ocean of thy love,
We lose ourselves, in heaven above.

www.ingramcontent.com/pod-product-compliance
Lightning Source LLC
Chambersburg PA
CBHW021454080526
44588CB00009B/847